THE THIRTEEN COLONIES IN THE US:
3RD GRADE US HISTORY SERIES

SPEEDY
PUBLISHING

Speedy Publishing LLC
40 E. Main St. #1156
Newark, DE 19711
www.speedypublishing.com

Copyright 2015

The Thirteen Colonies were British colonies on the east coast of North America which had been founded between 1607 and 1732.

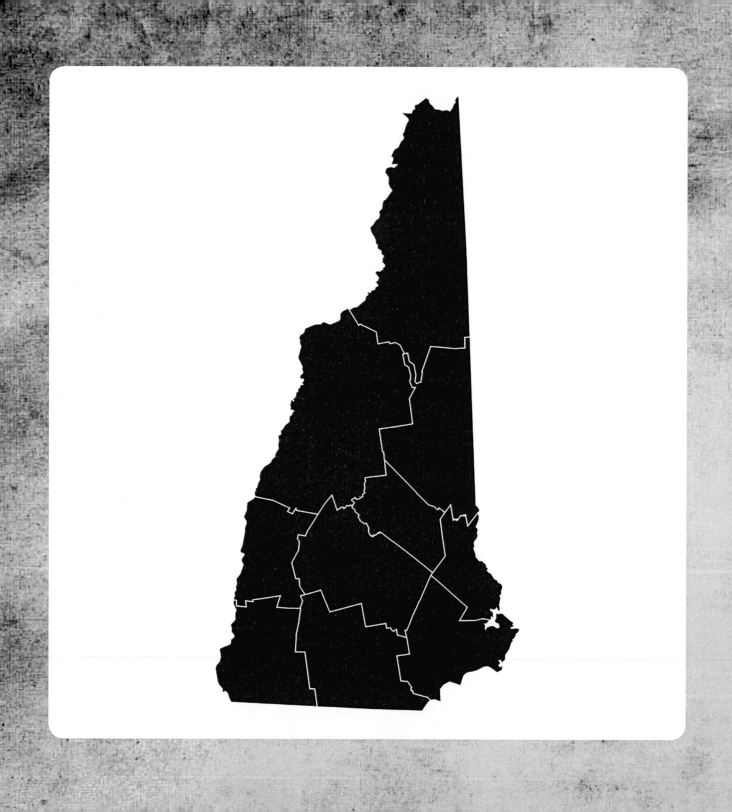

THE PROVINCE OF NEW HAMPSHIRE

was formally organized as an English royal colony on October 7, 1691.

The territory is now the U.S. state of New Hampshire.

THE PROVINCE OF MASSACHUSETTS BAY

was chartered on October 7, 1691. The name Massachusetts comes from the Massachusett, an Algonquian tribe.

COLONY OF RHODE ISLAND AND PROVIDENCE PLANTATIONS

was established on the east coast of North America. Providence Plantations was an American colony of English settlers founded in 1636 by Roger Williams.

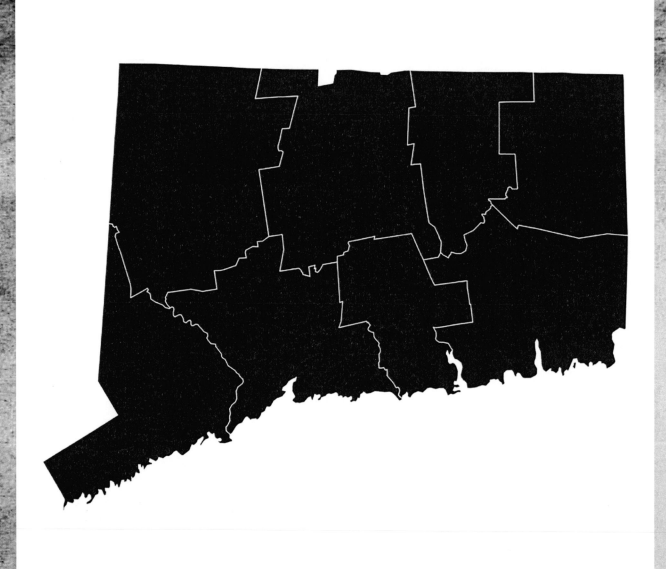

CONNECTICUT COLONY

originally known as the River Colony, it was organized on March 3, 1636. The colony was later the scene of a bloody and raging Pequot War.

PROVINCE OF NEW YORK

was an English and later British crown territory. The Province of New York was divided into twelve counties on November 1, 1683.

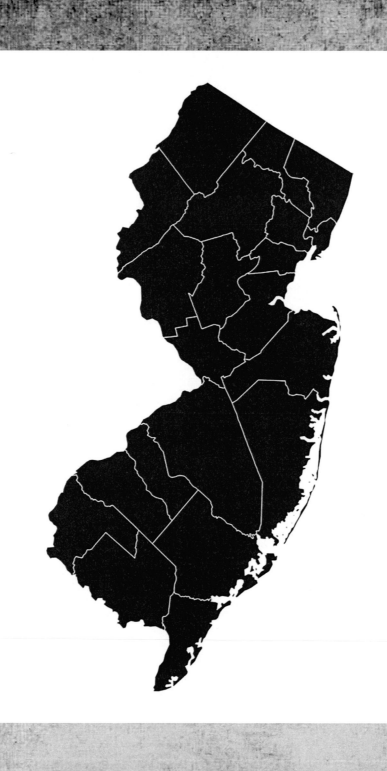

PROVINCE OF NEW JERSEY

was one of the Middle Colonies of Colonial America. The Province of New Jersey was originally settled in the 1610s as part of the colony of New Netherland.

PROVINCE OF PENNSYLVANIA

was founded in English North America on March 4, 1681. The Province of Pennsylvania was one of the two major restoration colonies.

DELAWARE COLONY

was founded in 1638 by Peter Minuit. The Delaware Colony was divided into three counties in 1682 including New Castle, Sussex, and Kent.

PROVINCE OF MARYLAND

was an English and later British colony in North America. The Maryland Colony was founded by Cecil Calvert, Lord Baltimore and others in 1633 at Baltimore.

COLONY AND DOMINION OF VIRGINIA

was the first English colony in the world. The Virginia Colony was founded by John Smith and other colonists in 1607.

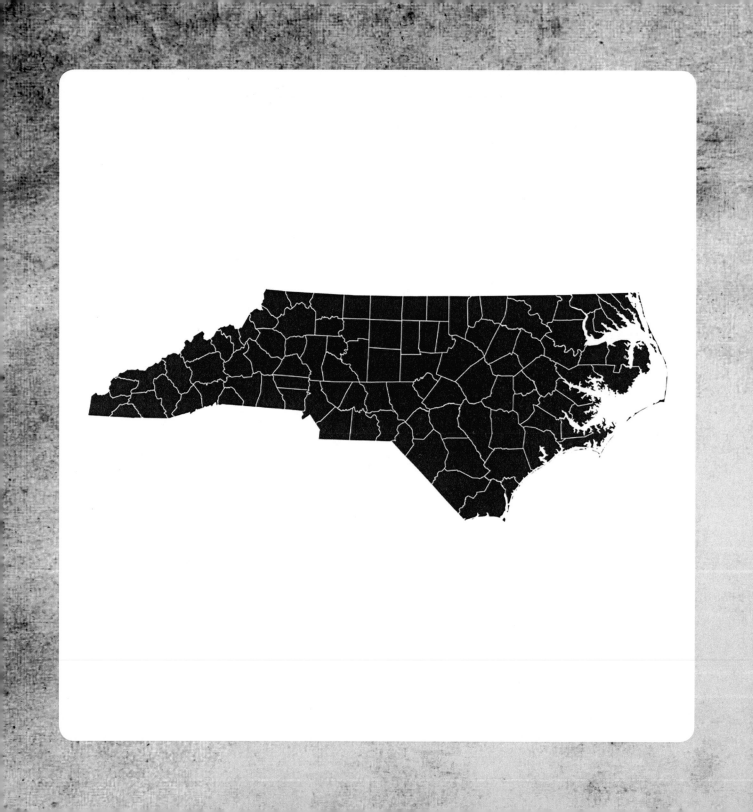

PROVINCE OF NORTH CAROLINA

was founded in 1653. Carolina
is a word derived from the Latin
name for Charles, 'Carolus'.

PROVINCE OF SOUTH CAROLINA

was founded in 1633 under
the Charter of Carolina. In 1729
the South Carolina Colony
became a royal colony.

PROVINCE OF GEORGIA

was founded in 1732 by several colonists including James Oglethorpe. The Georgia Colony was one of the Southern colonies in British America.

A Map of the
UNITED STATES
OF
AMERICA,
with Part of the
ADJOINING PROVINCES
from the latest Authorities.

British Statute Miles.

84096646R00020

Made in the USA
San Bernardino, CA
04 August 2018